CAROL ANN DUFFY was Poet Laureate of the United Kingdom for a decade from 2009 to 2019. Her poetry has received many awards, including the Signal Prize for Children's Verse, the Whitbread, Forward and T. S. Eliot Prizes, and the Lannan and E. M. Forster Awards in America. She won the PEN Pinter Prize in 2012, and was appointed DBE in 2015. In 2021, she was awarded the International Golden Wreath for lifetime achievement in poetry.

ELEGIES

Carol Ann Duffy

PICADOR

First published 2023 by Picador
an imprint of Pan Macmillan
The Smithson, 6 Briset Street, London EC1M 5NR
EU representative: Macmillan Publishers Ireland Ltd, 1st Floor,
The Liffey Trust Centre, 117–126 Sheriff Street Upper,
Dublin 1, DO1 YC43
Associated companies throughout the world
www.panmacmillan.com

ISBN 978-1-5290-9688-0

Printed and bound by CPI Group (UK) Ltd, Croydon, CR0 4YY

im Eugene Duffy

1962–2022

Contents

Whoever She Was   1

Liverpool Echo   3

Letters from Deadmen   4

And Then What   6

Sanctuary   7

Père Lachaise   10

Dream of a Lost Friend   12

Prayer   14

Anne Hathaway   15

Mrs Lazarus   16

Death and the Moon   19

Elegy   21

Vigil   22

Water   24

Last Post   25

Cold   27

Winter's Tale   28

Snow   29

The Dead   30

Sung   31

Premonitions   32

The Pendle Witches   34

Liverpool   36

Pathway   37

The Rain   39

Clerk of Hearts   41

Richard   42

Wedding Ring   43

Gardening   44

Long Table   45

How Death Comes   48

Before   50

Daughter   54

Whoever She Was

They see me always as a flickering figure
on a shilling screen. Not real. My hands,
still wet, sprout wooden pegs. I smell the apples
burning as I hang the washing out.
Mummy, say the little voices of the ghosts
of children on the telephone. Mummy.

A row of paper dollies, cleaning wounds
or boiling eggs for soldiers. The chant
of magic words repeatedly. I do not know.
Perhaps tomorrow. If we're very good.
The film is on a loop. Six silly ladies
torn in half by baby fists. When they
think of me, I'm bending over them at night,
to kiss. Perfume. Rustle of silk. Sleep tight.

Where does it hurt? A scrap of echo clings
to the bramble bush. My maiden name
sounds wrong. This was the playroom.
I turn it over on a clumsy tongue. Again.
These are the photographs. Making masks
from turnips in the candlelight. In case they come.

Whoever she was, forever their wide eyes watch her
as she shapes a church and steeple in the air.
She cannot be myself and yet I have a box
of dusty presents to confirm that she was here.
You remember the little things. Telling stories
or pretending to be strong. Mummy's never wrong.
You open your dead eyes to look in the mirror
which they are holding to your mouth.

1985

Liverpool Echo

Pat Hodges kissed you once, although quite shy,
in sixty-two. Small crowds in Mathew Street
endure rain for the echo of a beat,
as if nostalgia means you did not die.

Inside phone-booths loveless ladies cry
on Merseyside. Their faces show defeat.
An ancient jukebox blares out Ain't She Sweet
in Liverpool, which cannot say goodbye.

Here everybody has an anecdote
of how they met you, were the best of mates.
The seagulls circle round a ferry-boat

out on the river, where it's getting late.
Like litter on the water, people float
outside the Cavern in the rain. And wait.

1985

Letters from Deadmen

Beneath the earth a perfect femur glows. I recall
a little pain and then a century of dust. Observe my
    anniversary,
place purple violets tenderly before the urn. You must.
No one can hear the mulching of the heart, which
    thrummed
with blood or drummed with love. Perhaps, by now,
your sadness will be less. Unless you still remember me.

I flung silver pigeons to grey air with secret messages
for men I had not met. Do they ever mention me
at work and was there weeping in the crematorium?
Dear wife, dear child, I hope you leave my room
exactly as it was. The pipe, the wireless and, of course,
the cricket photographs. They say we rest in peace.

Ash or loam. Scattered or slowly nagged by worms. I lie
above my parents in the family plot and I fit neatly
in a metal cask in ever-loving memory of myself.
They parted his garments, casting lots upon them
what every man should take. A crate of stout.
Small talk above the salmon sandwiches. Insurance men.

But here you cannot think. The voice-box imitates
the skeletons of leaves. Words snail imperceptibly and
        soundless
in the soil. Dear love, remember me. Give me biography
beyond these simple dates. Were there psalms and hired
        limousines?
All this eternally before my final breath and may
this find you as it leaves me here. Eventually.

1985

And Then What

Then with their hands they would break bread
wave choke phone thump thread

Then with their tired hands slump
at a table holding their head

Then with glad hands hold other hands
or stroke brief flesh in a kind bed

Then with their hands on the shovel
they would bury their dead.

1985

Sanctuary

This morning you are not incurable, not yet, can walk
with your disease inside you, at its centre
your small pearl of hope, along the entrance path
where tall, cool pillars hold the sky. Ahead,
the archway, white, benevolent; calm doctors
who will dress you in clean robes. Now you cry
tears you have not wept for years. Relief.

Already, being here, you half believe, arriving
in Reception, acquiescent, giving your old clothes
up to the flames, giving your name. *Thank you,
yes, yes,* the anxious words like worry beads.
You will do as you are told, anything, accept
that the waters are holy, work wonders;
for a perfect fleshy shell exchange a golden ear.

You're sick. This placid world of thoughtful space,
philosophy, design, has taken you in. Forget.
Forget how you came here, what suffering
you endured to wait in the Circular Cure Centre
for a nurse, your heart reciting its own small number.
I want to be well, recall this treatment miles away,
pass pain on the street like a stranger. Please.

In the Library your shaking hand takes up a book,
thumbs miracles. These men were saved, prescriptions
scrawled upon their dreams. You read of venom,
oil, cream, a rooster's blood. Later your shadow
precedes you into the Chamber of Dreams. You'll dream
about yourself, chant your therapy as dawn arrives
with light for the blind stone eyes of statues.

Breathe in. Out. In. Sometimes you wake in darkness,
holding your own hand as if you will stay forever.
Think again. The months flew, that year in the Sanctuary
when you were cured. Remember a fool's face
pulling a tongue in a mirror, your dedication
carved in the Temple of Tributes. Its blatant lie
blushed on marble, one sunset as you died elsewhere.

1987

Père Lachaise

Along the ruined avenues the long gone lie
under the old stones. For 10 francs, a map unravels
the crumbling paths which lead to the late great.
A silent town. A vast, perplexing pause.

The living come, murmuring with fresh flowers, their
    maps
fluttering like white flags in the slight breeze.
April. Beginning of spring. Lilies for Oscar,
one red rose for Colette. Remembrance. Do not forget.

Turn left for Seurat, Chopin, Proust, and Gertrude Stein
with nothing more to say. Below the breathing trees
a thousand lost talents dream into dust; decay
into largely familiar names for a stranger's bouquet.

Forever dead. Say these words and let their meaning
dizzy you like the scent of innumerable petals
here in Père Lachaise. The sad tourists stand
by the graves, reciting the titles of poems, paintings,
    songs,

things which have brought them here for the afternoon.
We thread our way through the cemetery, misquoting
or humming quietly and almost comforted.
Two young men embrace near Piaf's tomb.

Dream of a Lost Friend

You were dead, but we met, dreaming,
before you had died. Your name, twice,
then you turned, pale, unwell. *My dear,
my dear, must this be?* A public building
where I've never been, and, on the wall,
an AIDS poster. Your white lips. *Help me.*

We embraced, standing in a long corridor
which harboured a fierce pain neither of us felt yet.
The words you spoke were frenzied prayers
to Chemistry; or you laughed, a child-man's laugh,
innocent, hysterical, out of your skull. *It's only
a dream*, I heard myself saying, *only a bad dream.*

Some of our best friends nurture a virus, an idle,
charmed, purposeful enemy, and it dreams
they are dead already. In fashionable restaurants,
over the crudités, the healthy imagine a time
when all these careful moments will be dreamed
and dreamed again. *You look well. How do you feel?*

Then, as I slept, you backed away from me, crying
and offering a series of dates for lunch, waving.
I missed your funeral, I said, knowing you couldn't hear
at the end of the corridor, thumbs up, acting.
Where there's life . . . Awake, alive, for months I think of
you
almost hopeful in a bad dream where you were long
dead.

1990

Prayer

Some days, although we cannot pray, a prayer
utters itself. So, a woman will lift
her head from the sieve of her hands and stare
at the minims sung by a tree, a sudden gift.

Some nights, although we are faithless, the truth
enters our hearts, that small familiar pain;
then a man will stand stock-still, hearing his youth
in the distant Latin chanting of a train.

Pray for us now. Grade I piano scales
console the lodger looking out across
a Midlands town. Then dusk, and someone calls
a child's name as though they named their loss.

Darkness outside. Inside, the radio's prayer –
Rockall. Malin. Dogger. Finisterre.

1990

14

Anne Hathaway

'Item I gyve unto my wief my second best bed . . .'
(from Shakespeare's will)

The bed we loved in was a spinning world
of forests, castles, torchlight, clifftops, seas
where he would dive for pearls. My lover's words
were shooting stars which fell to earth as kisses
on these lips; my body now a softer rhyme
to his, now echo, assonance; his touch
a verb dancing in the centre of a noun.
Some nights, I dreamed he'd written me, the bed
a page beneath his writer's hands. Romance
and drama played by touch, by scent, by taste.
In the other bed, the best, our guests dozed on,
dribbling their prose. My living laughing love –
I hold him in the casket of my widow's head
as he held me upon that next best bed.

1999

Mrs Lazarus

I had grieved. I had wept for a night and a day
over my loss, ripped the cloth I was married in
from my breasts, howled, shrieked, clawed
at the burial stones till my hands bled, retched
his name over and over again, dead, dead.

Gone home. Gutted the place. Slept in a single cot,
widow, one empty glove, white femur
in the dust, half. Stuffed dark suits
into black bags, shuffled in a dead man's shoes,
noosed the double knot of a tie round my bare neck,

gaunt nun in the mirror, touching herself. I learnt
the Stations of Bereavement, the icon of my face
in each bleak frame; but all those months
he was going away from me, dwindling
to the shrunk size of a snapshot, going,

going. Till his name was no longer a certain spell
for his face. The last hair on his head
floated out from a book. His scent went from the house.
The will was read. See, he was vanishing
to the small zero held by the gold of my ring.

Then he was gone. Then he was legend, language;
my arm on the arm of the schoolteacher – the shock
of a man's strength under the sleeve of his coat –
along the hedgerows. But I was faithful
for as long as it took. Until he was memory.

So I could stand that evening in the field
in a shawl of fine air, healed, able
to watch the edge of the moon occur to the sky
and a hare thump from a hedge; then notice
the village men running towards me, shouting,

behind them the women and children, barking dogs,
and I knew. I knew by the sly light
on the blacksmith's face, the shrill eyes
of the barmaid, the sudden hands bearing me
into the hot tang of the crowd parting before me.

He lived. I saw the horror on his face.
I heard his mother's crazy song. I breathed
his stench; my bridegroom in his rotting shroud,
moist and dishevelled from the grave's slack chew,
croaking his cuckold name, disinherited, out of his time.

1999

Death and the Moon

i.m. Adrian Henri

The moon is nearer than where death took you
at the end of the old year. Cold as cash
in the sky's dark pocket, its hard old face
is gold as a mask tonight. I break the ice
over the fish in my frozen pond, look up
as the ghosts of my wordless breath reach
for the stars. If I stood on the tip of my toes
and stretched, I could touch the edge of the moon.

I stooped at the lip of your open grave
to gather a fistful of earth, hard rain,
tough confetti, and tossed it down. It stuttered
like morse on the wood over your eyes, your tongue,
your soundless ears. Then as I slept my living sleep
the ground gulped you, swallowed you whole,
and though I was there when you died,
in the red cave of your widow's unbearable cry,

and measured the space between last words
and silence, I cannot say where you are. Unreachable
by prayer, even if poems are prayers. Unseeable
in the air, even if souls are stars. I turn
to the house, its windows tender with light, the moon,
surely, only as far again as the roof. The goldfish
are tongues in the water's mouth. The black night
is huge, mute, and you are further forever than that.

2002

20

Elegy

Who'll know then, when they walk by the grave
where your bones will be brittle things – this bone here
that swoops away from your throat, and this,
which perfectly fits the scoop of my palm, and these
which I count with my lips, and your skull,
which blooms on the pillow now, and your fingers,
beautiful in their little rings – that love, which wanders
    history,
singled you out in your time?

                Love loved you best; lit you
with a flame, like talent, under your skin; let you
move through your days and nights, blessed in your flesh,
blood, hair, as though they were lovely garments
you wore to pleasure the air. Who'll guess, if they read
your stone, or press their thumbs to the scars
of your dates, that were I alive, I would lie on the grass
above your bones till I mirrored your pose, your infinite
    grace?

2005

Vigil

Manchester Pride, 2010

When you were,
no one could hold a candle to you.
Tonight, memory's small flames,
which scald the hands with wax tears,
are tongues, uttering
your name in light.

You burned bright, illuminating
the vigilance of science,
the grace of tolerance.
This silence now,
a deep warm gathering of breath
to blow out guttering words:
stigma, ignorance, hate.
Let them know death.

One lit taper kisses another,
contagious with fire,
and darkness glitters; brief flowers
each with their own smoke ghost.
They could be dancing, that close;
the living holding vigil
for the lost.

2010

Water

Your last word was *water*,
which I poured in a hospice plastic cup, held
to your lips – your small sip, half-smile, sigh –
then, in the chair beside you,

      fell asleep.

Fell asleep for three lost hours,
only to waken, thirsty, hear then see
a magpie warn in a bush outside –
dawn so soon – and swallow from your still-full cup.

Water. The times I'd call as a child
for a drink, till you'd come, sit on the edge
of the bed in the dark, holding my hand,
just as we held hands now and you died.

A good last word.
    Nights since I've cried, but gone
to my own child's side with a drink, watched
her gulp it down then sleep. *Water.*
What a mother brings
    through darkness still
to her parched daughter.

2011

Last Post

In all my dreams, before my helpless sight,
He plunges at me, guttering, choking, drowning.

If poetry could tell it backwards, true, begin
that moment shrapnel scythed you to the stinking mud . . .
but you get up, amazed, watch bled bad blood
run upwards from the slime into its wounds;
see lines and lines of British boys rewind
back to their trenches, kiss the photographs from home —
mothers, sweethearts, sisters, younger brothers
not entering the story now
to die and die and die.
Dulce – No – Decorum – No – Pro patria mori.
You walk away.

You walk away; drop your gun (fixed bayonet)
like all your mates do too —
Harry, Tommy, Wilfred, Edward, Bert —
and light a cigarette.
There's coffee in the square,
warm French bread,
and all those thousands dead

are shaking dried mud from their hair
and queueing up for home. Freshly alive,
a lad plays Tipperary to the crowd, released
from History; the glistening, healthy horses fit for
    heroes, kings.

You lean against a wall,
your several million lives still possible
and crammed with love, work, children, talent, English
    beer, good food.
You see the poet tuck away his pocket-book and smile.

If poetry could truly tell it backwards,
then it would.

2011

Cold

It felt so cold, the snowball which wept in my hands,
and when I rolled it along in the snow, it grew
till I could sit on it, looking back at the house,
where it was cold when I woke in my room, the windows
blind with ice, my breath undressing itself on the air.
Cold, too, embracing the torso of snow which I lifted up
in my arms to build a snowman, my toes, burning, cold
in my winter boots; my mother's voice calling me in
from the cold. And her hands were cold from peeling
and pooling potatoes into a bowl, stooping to cup
her daughter's face, a kiss for both cold cheeks, my cold
    nose.
But nothing so cold as the February night I opened the
    door
in the Chapel of Rest where my mother lay, neither
    young, nor old,
where my lips, returning her kiss to her brow, knew the
    meaning of cold.

2011

Winter's Tale

Tell she is well in these arms;
synonymous, her heartbeat to mine;
the world a little room; undone
all hurt; her inbreath, breath,
love where death, where harm, hope,
flesh where stone; my line – *O*
she's warm! – charm, blessing, prayer,
spell; outwith dream, without time;
enchantment tell, garden from grave
to garland her; above these worms,
violet, oxlip, primrose, columbine;
she wakes, moves, prompted by her name.

2011

Snow

Then all the dead opened their cold palms
and released the snow; slow, slant, silent,
a huge unsaying, it fell, torn language, settled;
the world to be locked, local; unseen,
fervent earthbound bees around a queen.
The river grimaced and was ice.

                        Go nowhere –
thought the dead, using the snow –
but where you are, offering the flower of your breath
to the white garden, or seeds to birds
from your living hand. You cannot leave.
Tighter and tighter, the beautiful snow
holds the land in its fierce embrace.
It is like death, but it is not death; lovelier.
Cold, inconvenienced, late, what will you do now
with the gift of your left life?

2011

The Dead

They're very close to us, the dead;
us in our taxis, them in their hearses,
waiting for the lights to change.
We give them precedence.

So close to us, unknown on television;
dead from hunger, earthquake, war,
suicide bomber, tsunami.
We count the numbers.

The famous dead – a double glamour –
we buy their music, movies, memoirs.
O! Elizabeth Taylor as Cleopatra
in glorious technicolor.

In Venice, we glimpse the dead
drift to the island cemetery across the lagoon.
We float our gondolas along the green canals
and do not die.

2011

Sung

Now only words in a song,
no more than a name
on a stone,
and that well overgrown –
MAR– –ORIS– –;

and wind though a ruined croft,
the door an appalled mouth,
the window's eye put out;

hours and wishes and trysts
less than shadows of bees on grass,
ghosts that did dance, did kiss . . .

those who would gladly die for love long dead –
a skull for a bonnie head –
and love a simile, a rose, red, red.

2011

Premonitions

We first met when your last breath
cooled in my palm like an egg;
you dead, and a thrush outside
sang it was morning.
I backed out of the room, feeling
the flowers freshen and shine in my arms.

The night before, we met again, to unsay
unbearable farewells, to see
our eyes brighten with re-strung tears.
O I had my sudden wish –
though I barely knew you –
to stand at the door of your house,
feeling my heartbeat calm,
as they carried you in, home, home and healing.
Then slow weeks, removing the wheelchair, the drugs,
the oxygen mask and tank, the commode,
the appointment cards,
until it was summer again
and I saw you open the doors to the grace of your garden.

Strange and beautiful to see
the flowers close to their own premonitions,
the grass sweeten and cool and green
where a bee swooned backwards out of a rose.
There you were,
a glass of lemony wine in each hand,
walking towards me always, your magnolia tree
marrying itself to the May air.

How you talked! And how I listened,
spellbound, humbled, daughterly,
to your tall tales, your wise words,
the joy of your accent, unenglish, dancey, humorous;
watching your ash hair flare and redden,
the loving litany of who we had been
making me place my hands in your warm hands,
younger than mine are now.
Then time only the moon. And the balm of dusk.
And you my mother.

2011

The Pendle Witches

One voice for ten dragged this way once
by superstition, ignorance.
Thou shalt not suffer a witch to live.

Witch: female, cunning, manless, old,
daughter of such, of evil faith;
in the murk of Pendle Hill, a crone.

Here, heavy storm-clouds, ill-will brewed,
over fields, fells, farms, blighted woods.
On the wind's breath, curse of crow and rook.

From poverty, no poetry
but weird spells, half-prayer, half-threat;
sharp pins in little dolls of death.

At daylight's gate, the things we fear
darken and form. That tree, that rock,
a slattern's shape ropes the devil's dog.

Something upholds us in its palm –
landscape, history, sudden time –
and, above, the gormless witness moon

below which Demdike, Chattox, shrieked,
like hags, unloved, an underclass,
eyes red, gobs gummed, unwell, unfed.

But that was then – when difference
made ghouls of neighbours; children begged,
foul, feral, filthy, in their cowls.

Grim skies, the grey remorse of rain;
cloudbreak, sunset's shame; four seasons,
turning centuries, in Lancashire,

away from Castle, Jury, Judge,
huge crowd, rough rope, short drop, no grave;
only future tourists who might grieve.

2014

Liverpool

The Cathedral bell, tolled, could never tell;
nor the Liver Birds, mute in their stone spell;
or the Mersey, though seagulls wailed, cursed, overhead,
in no language for the slandered dead . . .

not the raw, red throat of the Kop, keening,
or the cops' words, censored of meaning;
not the clock, slow handclapping the coroner's deadline,
or the memo to Thatcher, or the tabloid headline . . .

but fathers told of their daughters; the names of sons
on the lips of their mothers were prayers; lost ones
honoured for bitter years by orphan, cousin, wife –
not a matter of football, but of life.

Over this great city, light after long dark;
and truth, the sweet silver song of a lark.

2014

Pathway

I saw my father walking in my garden
and where he walked,

                    the garden lengthened

to a changing mile
which held all seasons of the year.
He did not see me, staring from my window,
a child's star face, hurt light from stricken time,
and he had treaded spring and summer grasses
before I thought to stir, follow him.

Autumn's cathedral, open to the weather, rose
high above, flawed amber, gorgeous ruin; his shadow
stretched before me, *cappa magna*,
my own, obedient, trailed like a nun.
He did not turn. I heard the rosaries of birds.
The trees, huge doors, swung open and I knelt.

He stepped into a silver room of cold;
a narrow bed of ice stood glittering,
and though my father wept, he could not leave,
but had to strip, then shiver in his shroud,

till winter palmed his eyes for frozen bulbs,
or sliced his tongue, a silencing of worms.

The moon a simple headstone without words.

2014

The Rain

That time will come
                    when it starts to rain
in your quiet room,
grief researching you;
its curious, small thumbs on your closed eyes,
on your pulse;
or smudging the ink of this,
or dipping into that glass of wine.
The moment stammers.

Too intimate,
                    relentless biographer
poring over your ruined books,
persistent, till every surface is soaked
as though you lamented, night and day,
for a lifetime;
or were penned, invented.
Leave the room to the rain . . .

the clock's hands float

                  on its drowned face
and photographs swim from their frames
and hours are sorrow, rain, rain, sorrow . . .
why climb the stairs to lie down there,
be drenched, tasted, known
by the pitiless rain?
You have dead parents.

2018

Clerk of Hearts

As they step from the path onto the boats,
I am there at my place under the trees,
listing the Categories. *Humility. Shame.*

My dealings with life have been so long ago,
I imagine I resemble shadow or watermark.
I am unanswered prayer, like poetry. *Dread.*

Whatever I did – it might have been that – now,
I watch each one depart, perceive their hearts;
old diaries I read at a glance. *Acceptance. Disdain.*

They will forget, but I take Time, devoted,
clerk of hearts. Sometimes I stand on the bridge
as they drift away, being more and more dead . . .

a kingfisher arrowing upriver, joy as colour;
then thunder above, a boiling of last words,
and their crafts vanishing into the heavy rain.

2018

Richard

My bones, scripted in light, upon cold soil,
a human braille. My skull, scarred by a crown,
emptied of history. Describe my soul
as incense, votive, vanishing; your own
the same. Grant me the carving of my name.

These relics, bless. Imagine you re-tie
a broken string and on it thread a cross,
the symbol severed from me when I died.
The end of time – an unknown, unfelt loss –
unless the Resurrection of the Dead . . .

or I once dreamed of this, your future breath
in prayer for me, lost long, forever found;
or sensed you from the backstage of my death,
as Kings glimpse shadows on a battleground.

2018

Wedding Ring

When I eased it from her finger
and onto my own,
I married her absence;
the years between her passing and mine.
The small *o* in love and loss.

2018

Gardening

I watched my parents gardening in death;
she knelt in green shade with a trowel;
he stood on wooden steps to hang a basket,
trailing black-eyed susan vine, sweet alyssum
and million bells; his shape's dark shroud
dropped on the lawn.

If they had turned
to glimpse me at the window, staring down,
they would have thought they'd seen a ghost,
waving . . . but when I ran downstairs, outside,
they would have gone.

                They could not look, I knew,
must garden still, until a frost came on,
engraving all they planted, all they grew.

2018

Long Table

It is a long table
where the folks sit, supping
their ale or sipping wine;
friends of mine.

They gather in shadow,
candlelight; heads haloed
as though painted in oils;
singled all.

Their voices lift and fall,
a blare of merriment,
a blur of soft prayer;
beloved there.

My Green Man, grey-haired now,
yet mirthful in sorrow;
as winter sun eases
ice from trees.

Our Lady of Good Cheer,
garlanded; the flowers
and leaves of the old year
in her hair.

And the lasses and lads
whose faces flare brightest
at the feast, in uplift
for youth's gift.

Our dead waver outside,
tethered by memory;
their own darkness is light
seen too late.

If they could live again
they would listen, even
to silent drifting snow;
its kind *No*.

But the fire chortles here,
rubbing its hands of flame,
and we are carousing
in rough song;

blessed in the small hours –
where cold bites at the house,
though cannot enter yet –
and well-met.

2018

How Death Comes

(Anon, 13th century)

When my eyes film
And my ears hum
And my nose chills
And my tongue curls
And my mouth grins
And my drool runs
And my lips crack
And my arse cacks
And my hair moults
And my heart jolts
And my hands wizen
And my feet stiffen –
It's all too late, too late,
when the cart's at the gate.

Then I shall shift
From kip to floor
From floor to shroud
From shroud to door
From door to crate
From crate to pit
And the pit will shut.
Then I will sprout pissabeds among moss
And I won't give a toss.

2018

Before

Before the ox treads on your tongue,
say what is;
           how the numerous greens of this garden
lean in, numinous. When it rains,
you should be part, yearning with all five senses,
   too aware.
But your soul is; your soul,
                which after keeping yourself
   to yourself
for a matter of time,
          took up residence,
and wanders the garden now; invisibly green.

*

Before the thistle hooks to your lip,
utter a verb;
          the white flowers you planted pine with love
for the gloaming; the gloaming itself
seems in love
        with its name.

The hour when things come as close to you

                                as they dare,

brushing your lips with their nouns.

*

Before the sear of the sun, the smear of the moon,
are the same to you,

                what's to be said?
The sun on the lake and the moon on the lake
are major, minor, music

                as light,
and words modest, shy, shying away;
bats skimming the water's skin.

*

Before a stone stoppers your mouth,

                        describe
how this evening's sky is slowly

                  yawning

                      the stars;
and colour withdraws, joy

                in reverse; wiser.

*

Before the yellowy, bell-embellished air cannot be
breathed, heard, seen, tell
                            the time;
a moment reaching for only you
                                    over the fields;
trembling the wine in your glass.

*

Before just moss
reads the braille of your dates,
fill in the hyphen-space;
                            linking the nothing before
to the nothing that waits.

*

Before a spade shovels the latin dark,
allow that the priest of a tree
would have heard your wedding vows,
had you knelt.

*

Before God is eternally not,
say your prayers; credit
their sweetly human powers.

*

Before the chrism's thumbed on your brow,
say what you meant to say before.

*

Before before the ox treads on your tongue.

*

*

*

2020

Daughter

Your mother's daughter, you set your face
to the road
that ran by the river; behind you, the castle,
its mute ballroom,
lowered flag. Stoic, your profile a head on a coin,
you followed the hearse
through sorrow's landscape – a farmer, stood
on a tractor,
lifting his tweed cap; a group of anglers
shouldering their rods.
And now the villagers, silently raising
their mobile phones.
Then babies held aloft in the towns, to one day
be told they were there.

But you had your mother's eyes, as a horse ran free
in a field;
a pheasant flared from a hedge
like a thrown bouquet;
journeying on through a harvest of strange love.
How they craned to glimpse their lives again
in her death; reminded
of Time's relentless removals, their own bereavements,
as she passed.
The uplift of the high bridge over a dazzle of water;
a sense of ascending
into anointing light which dissolved into cloud.
Nine more slow grey miles to the Old Town; the last mile
a royal mile,

where they gathered ten-deep as your mother showed you
what she had meant.
Nightfall and downpour near London. Even the
    motorways paused;
thousands of headlights in rain
as you shadowed her still; smatterings of applause
from verges and bridges.
Soon enough they would come to know this had long been
the Age of Grief;
that History was ahead of them. The crown of ice melting
on the roof of the world.
Tonight, childhood's palace; the iPhone torches linking
    back
to medieval flame.
So you slowed and arrived with her, her only daughter,
and only her daughter.

2022